to my
Daddy

from

_____

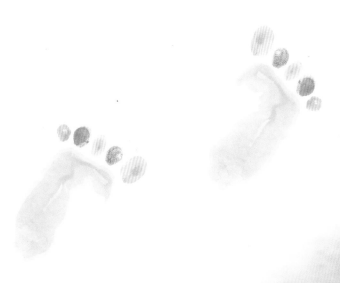

Will you teach me Daddy
and help me to know,
why the top of the mountains
are covered with snow?

And can you tell me Daddy
why you are so tall,
and why are the leaves
beginning to fall?

You could read with me Daddy,
please help me to read.
We can learn about plants,
how they grow from a seed.

And what is that word Daddy?
Can you help me to say
spaghetti and meatballs
and Thanksgiving Day?

Wouldn't it be fun Daddy,
to learn about stars
and that faraway place
that grownups call Mars?

See, I want to know Daddy
what all I can be,
a fireman, a doctor,
an astronaut, that's me!

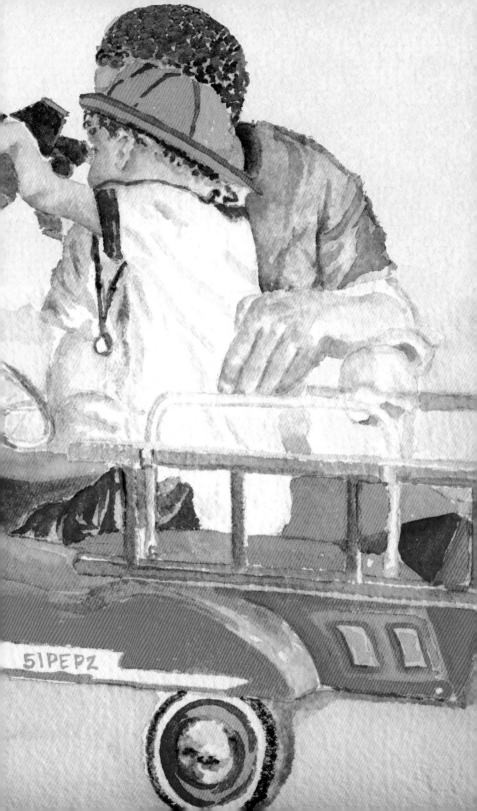

And if you teach me Daddy,
someday you will see
that when I grow up
you'll be so proud of me.

So tell me Daddy,
tell me all that is true.

And teach me Daddy
because I love you.

I am _____ years old.

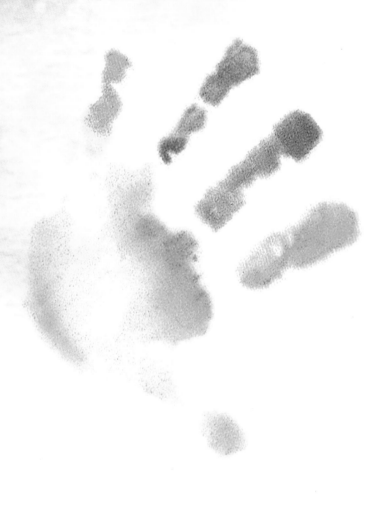

Trace your child's hand

Trace your child's foot